USING BEAKERS AND GRADUATED CYLINDERS

Lorijo Metz

PowerKiDS press.

New York

To Kathleen Stevens, may the volume of your coffee always be large

Published in 2013 by The Rosen Publishing Group, Inc.
29 East 21st Street, New York, NY 10010

First Edition

Editor: Amelie von Zumbusch
Book Design: Kate Laczynski

Photo Credits: Cover Hill Street Studios/Getty Images; p. 4 Purestock/Getty Images; p. 5 R. Gino Santa Maria/Shutterstock.com; p. 6 Ann Worthy/Shutterstock.com; p. 7 (top) Hemera/Thinkstock; p. 7 (bottom) PhotoObjects.net/Thinkstock; p. 9 RGtimeline/Shutterstock.com; p. 10 Creatas Images/Creatas/Thinkstock; p. 11 © iStockphoto.com/Tommounsey; p 12 (both) Charles D. Winters/Photo Researchers/Getty Images; p. 13 Monkey Business Images/Shutterstock.com; p. 14 Jupiterimages/Goodshoot/Thinkstock; p. 15 (top) © iStockphoto.com/Deborah Cheramie; p. 15 (bottom) Jason Stitt/Shutterstock.com; p. 17 © iStockphoto.com/Nikada; pp. 18, 20 iStockphoto/Thinkstock; p. 19 (left) Africa Studio/Shutterstock.com; p. 19 (right) Darryl Brooks/Shutterstock.com; p. 21 Photo Researchers/Getty Images; p. 22 © iStockphoto.com/Ashok Rodrigues.

Library of Congress Cataloging-in-Publication Data

Metz, Lorijo.
  Using beakers and graduated cylinders / by Lorijo Metz. — 1st ed.
    p. cm. — (Science tools)
  Includes index.
  ISBN 978-1-4488-9685-1 (library binding) — ISBN 978-1-4488-9828-2 (pbk.) —
  ISBN 978-1-4488-9829-9 (6-pack)
  1. Scientific apparatus and instruments—Juvenile literature. 2. Volume (Cubic content)—Juvenile literature. I. Title.
  Q185.3.M48 2013
  681'.75—dc23
                                      2012029011

Manufactured in the United States of America

CPSIA Compliance Information: Batch #W13PK4: For Further Information contact Rosen Publishing, New York, New York at 1-800-237-9932

CONTENTS

Beakers and Graduated Cylinders

Cooks use special cups to measure dry ingredients, such as flour and sugar. For liquids, they use another type of measuring cup. Scientists are a bit like cooks, always mixing and measuring things for **experiments**. They also use special containers to measure and mix liquids. The most common of these are beakers and graduated cylinders.

These girls are using graduated cylinders for an experiment in their science class.

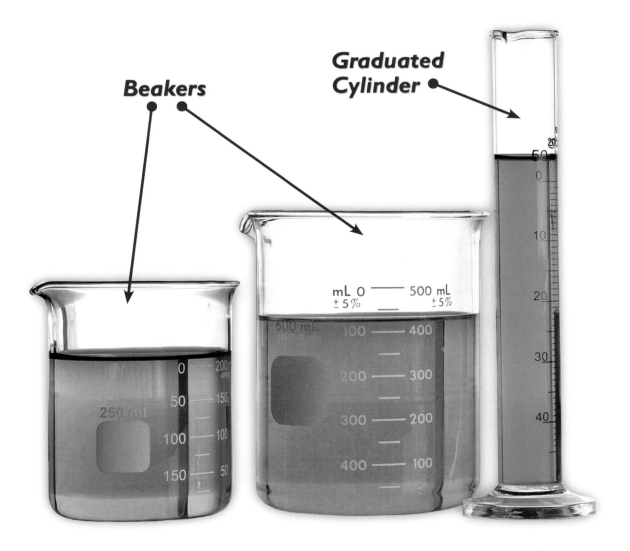

Beakers

Graduated Cylinder

Beakers look like big, clear, straight-sided glasses with lips for pouring. Graduated cylinders are tall, thin tubes. Both have lines on the side for measuring. Have you ever experimented with mixing liquids in class? If you have, chances are you have used a beaker.

Everything is made of **matter**, including you, oil, and even the steam that escapes from a teapot. **Volume** is the amount of space matter takes up. American cooks often measure the volume of liquids in ounces. Water that takes up a volume of 8 ounces is equal to 1 cup. Cups, pints, quarts, and gallons are all ways Americans describe the volume of liquids.

Cooks use liquid measuring cups to measure liquid ingredients, such as milk, cream, water, and oil.

Scientists use the metric system for measuring volume. Beakers and graduated cylinders are marked with milliliters, abbreviated "ml," and liters, abbreviated "l." One liter equals 1,000 milliliters. In general, scientists use beakers for mixing and graduated cylinders for more exact measurements.

In the United States, milk tends to be sold in gallons, half gallons, and quarts. A quart is one-quarter of a gallon.

250-ml beaker

120-ml beaker

100-ml beaker

50-ml beaker

The three main **states** of matter are solid, liquid, and gas. At high enough temperatures, even solids, such as rocks, will turn into liquids or gases.

How we measure matter depends on what state it is in. In its solid form, water is ice. You can figure out the volume of an ice cube if you know how long, wide, and tall it is.

Unlike solids, liquids take the shape of the container in which they are placed.

To find the volume of a liquid, such as water, you must place it in a container already measured for volume. Beakers and graduated cylinders are clear so scientists can see both the liquid and the volume measurements along the side.

Reading Beakers and Graduated Cylinders

Most beakers and graduated cylinders are marked in milliliters. Large beakers also show liters. To read them, you need to know the value of each measuring line.

Look carefully at the lines on the glass when you are measuring with a graduated cylinder.

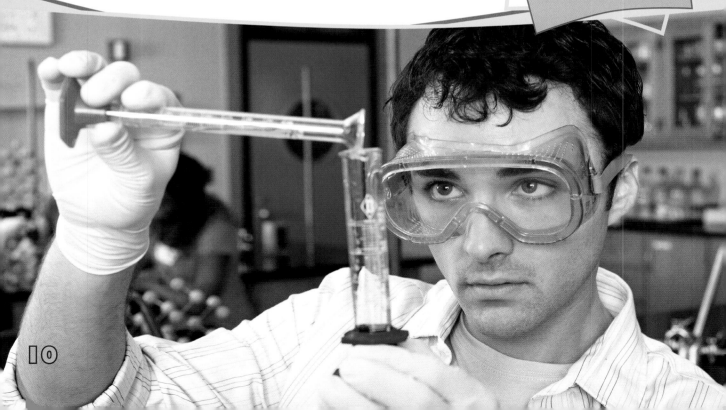

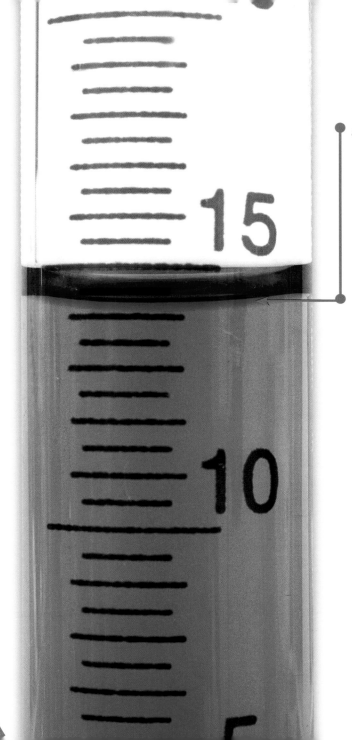

Meniscus

For example, a 30-ml cylinder may have numbered lines at 10, 20, and 30 ml. Between each graduated line are smaller lines, usually showing 1-ml increases.

In glass and plastic containers, liquids take on a curved appearance called a **meniscus**. To measure, place the cylinder or beaker on a flat surface and view the liquid at eye level. Measure the volume at the line the bottom of the meniscus falls closest to.

Displacement

Water level after displacement

Original water level

HOW WATER DISPLACEMENT WORKS

You can use these photos of a graduated cylinder before (left) and after (right) an object was placed in it to figure out the object's volume.

It is easy to find the volume of solids that you can measure the width, length, and height of. However, many solids have unusual shapes and are not easy to measure. To find the volume of these solids, you can use **displacement**. Displacement measures the volume of a solid by seeing how much liquid it displaces, or moves.

Fill a beaker or graduated cylinder half-full with water and note the volume level. Next, place your solid in the water. Note the new volume level of the water. To find the volume of the solid, subtract the first volume from the second volume.

You can use water displacement to compare the volumes of small objects. Do you think a grape or a raspberry has a bigger volume?

13

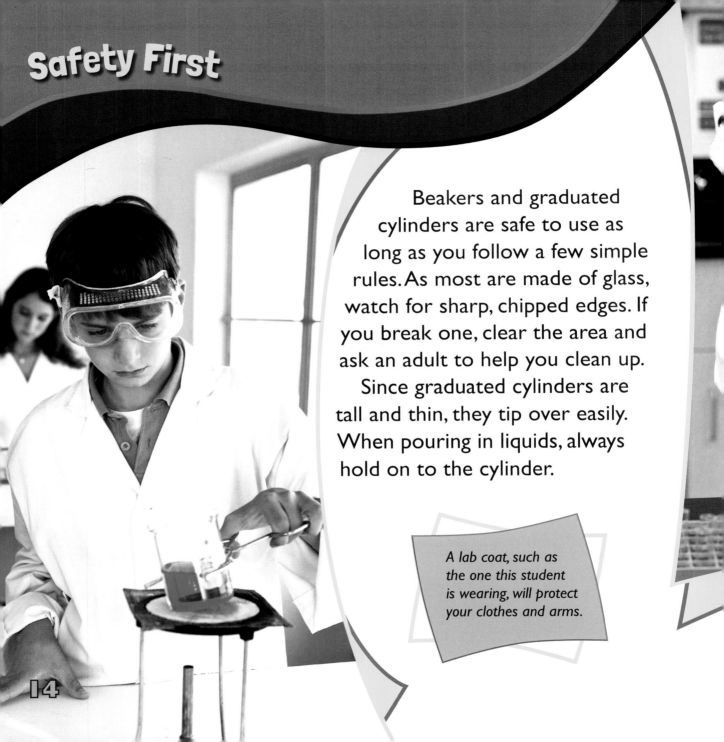

Safety First

Beakers and graduated cylinders are safe to use as long as you follow a few simple rules. As most are made of glass, watch for sharp, chipped edges. If you break one, clear the area and ask an adult to help you clean up.

Since graduated cylinders are tall and thin, they tip over easily. When pouring in liquids, always hold on to the cylinder.

A lab coat, such as the one this student is wearing, will protect your clothes and arms.

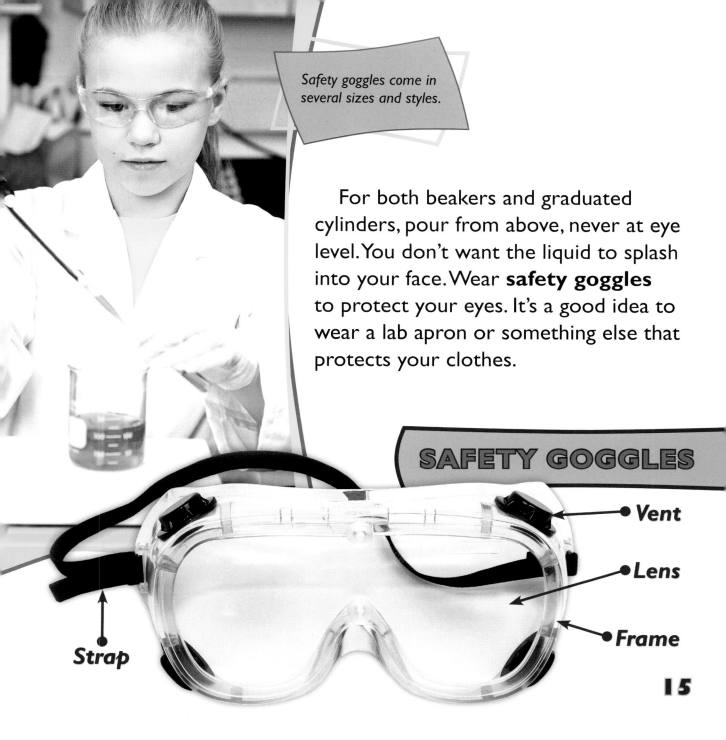

Safety goggles come in several sizes and styles.

For both beakers and graduated cylinders, pour from above, never at eye level. You don't want the liquid to splash into your face. Wear **safety goggles** to protect your eyes. It's a good idea to wear a lab apron or something else that protects your clothes.

SAFETY GOGGLES

Vent

Lens

Frame

Strap

Scientists tend to **observe** things and question how they work. Based on study, they form **hypotheses**, or guesses, to answer their questions. To test their hypotheses, they create experiments.

Experiments must be able to be repeated. Each time, only what you are testing should change. Therefore, the tools you use for your experiments must stay the same. Between experiments, thoroughly clean all tools, including beakers and graduated cylinders, and let them air dry. When measuring liquids, choose a graduated cylinder that is large enough to hold all the liquid but is not too large. In general, use beakers for mixing and graduated cylinders for measuring.

People who do experiments often work in groups. If you are working with a group, remember to discuss each step of the experiment with the rest of the group.

Studying Rainfall

Is there a lot of rain in the area where you live?

A rain gauge is a tool for collecting and measuring daily rainfall. Scientists who study weather use rain gauges to see patterns that help them **forecast**, or guess, how much rain will fall in a given month in an area.

To make your own simple rain gauge, use a beaker with a wide opening. Place it in a spot that is not covered.

A BEAKER RAIN GAUGE

The spot should be protected from the wind. Choose one time each day to write down, or **log**, the amount of rain collected. Empty your rain gauge between each measuring. Over time, see what patterns you notice.

250-ml beaker

200

150

250

100

50

● **Rain level (75 ml)**

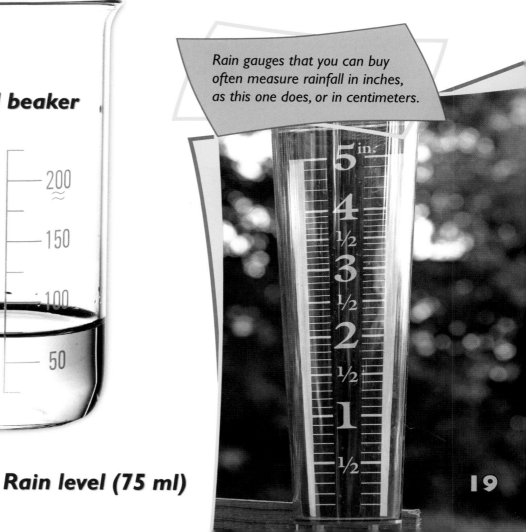

Rain gauges that you can buy often measure rainfall in inches, as this one does, or in centimeters.

5 in.

4

½

3

½

2

½

1

½

In the Laboratory

In **laboratories**, you will find many sizes of beakers and graduated cylinders. The scientists who work there know that it is important to be exact when mixing **chemicals**. The wrong amount can ruin an experiment. It can also be dangerous.

Students learn how to mix chemicals in chemistry classes.

Always work with an adult when experimenting with chemicals. When pouring chemicals into a beaker or graduated cylinder, pour slowly to avoid splashing and always wear safety goggles.

There is a saying that sometimes the simplest answer is the best one. Beakers and graduated cylinders are like that. They may be simple, but they are very useful tools!

You are going to test things to see if they will float in water. Below is what you need:

1. Four 500-ml beakers
2. Two graduated cylinders
3. One ice cube
4. One pebble
5. Vegetable oil
6. Corn syrup mixed with food coloring
7. A notebook and pencil to log your observations

List each thing on a separate line in your notebook. Write down if you think each will float or sink. Fill each beaker with 300 ml of water. Drop the ice cube in one beaker and the pebble in another. Use one graduated cylinder to measure out 40 ml of vegetable oil and the other to measure out 40 ml of corn syrup. Add each of these to a beaker. Observe and record which objects float.

GLOSSARY

chemicals (KEH-mih-kulz) Matter that can be mixed with other matter to cause changes.

displacement (dis-PLAYS-ment) Moving something out of the way.

experiments (ik-SPER-uh-ments) Actions or steps taken to learn more about something.

forecast (FOR-kast) To figure out when something will happen.

hypotheses (hy-PAH-theh-seez) Possible answers to problems.

laboratories (LA-bruh-tor-eez) Rooms in which scientists do tests.

log (LOG) To record day-to-day activities.

matter (MA-ter) Anything that has weight and takes up space.

meniscus (meh-NIS-kus) The curve at the top of a liquid in a container.

observe (ub-ZERV) To notice.

safety goggles (SAYF-tee GOG-elz) Glasses that protect the eyes.

states (STAYTS) Forms that matter can take, such as solid, liquid, or gas.

volume (VOL-yoom) The amount of space that matter takes up.

INDEX

WEBSITES

Due to the changing nature of Internet links, PowerKids Press has developed an online list of websites related to the subject of this book. This site is updated regularly. Please use this link to access the list:
www.powerkidslinks.com/scto/beak/